Who's in CONTROL?

Buffy Silverman

www.raintreepublishers.co.uk
Visit our website to find out more information about **Raintree** books.

To order:
 Phone 44 (0) 1865 888112
 Send a fax to 44 (0) 1865 314091
🖥 Visit the Raintree bookshop at **www.raintreepublishers.co.uk** to browse
our catalogue and order online.

First published in Great Britain by Raintree,
Halley Court, Jordan Hill, Oxford OX2 8EJ,
part of Harcourt Education.
Raintree is a registered trademark of Harcourt
Education Ltd.

Editorial: Louise Galpine and Harriet Milles
Design: Michelle Lisseter and Bigtop
Illustrations: Darren Lingard
Picture Research: Mica Brancic and Maria Joannou
Production: Camilla Crask

Originated by Modern Age
Printed and bound in China by WKT Company
Limited

10-digit ISBN 1 406 20474 9 (hardback)
13-digit ISBN 978 1 4062 0474 2
11 10 09 08 07
10 9 8 7 6 5 4 3 2 1

10-digit ISBN 1 406 20499 4 (paperback)
13-digit ISBN 978 1 4062 0499 5
11 10 09 08 07
10 9 8 7 6 5 4 3 2 1

**British Library
Cataloguing in Publication Data**
Silverman, Buffy
Who's in control? - (Fusion): Nervous system
612.8'2
A full catalogue record for this book is available from
the British Library.

Acknowledgements
The publishers would like to thank the following for
permission to reproduce photographs:
Alamy/Shotfile p. **20**; Corbis pp. **4–5** (Patrik
Giardino), **16** (Ed Bock), **23** (LucyNicholson/Reuters),
29; Getty Images pp. **8** (Iconica), **10** (Altrendo), **27**
(Bob Thomas), **29** (Imagebank); Harcourt Education
p. **28** (Jules Selmes); Masterfile pp. **6**, **15** (Graham
French); Science Photo Library pp. **24–25**.

Cover photograph of an MRI of the brain and spinal
column, reproduced with permission of Corbis
(Lester Lefkowitz).

Every effort has been made to contact copyright
holders of any material reproduced in this book. Any
omissions will be rectified in subsequent printings if
notice is given to the publishers.

The publishers would like to thank Nancy Harris and
Harold Pratt for their assistance with the preparation
of this book.

Disclaimer
All the Internet addresses (URLs) given in this book
were valid at the time of going to press. However,
due to the dynamic nature of the Internet, some
addresses may have changed, or sites may have
changed or ceased to exist since publication. While
the author and publishers regret any inconvenience
this may cause readers, no responsibility for any
such changes can be accepted by either the author
or the publishers.

It is recommended that adults supervise children on
the Internet.

Contents

Who's in control?   4

Body messengers   6

The coach   10

Control centre   14

The team   20

Move fast!   24

Learning to be your best   26

Brain bits   28

Glossary   30

Want to know more?   31

Index   32

Some words are printed in bold, **like this**. You can find out what they mean on page 30. You can also look in the box at the bottom of the page where they first appear.

Who's in control?

You are on the basketball court. A teammate catches the ball. You race down the court. Your teammate throws the ball to you. You reach out. You catch the ball! How do your legs know where to go? How do your hands know how to catch the ball?

It is your **brain** that tells your body what to do. Your brain controls your thoughts. Your brain controls your movements. First, your eyes see the ball. Your eyes send information to the brain. Then, your brain decides which muscles to move. Your legs run. Your hands reach out. You catch the ball!

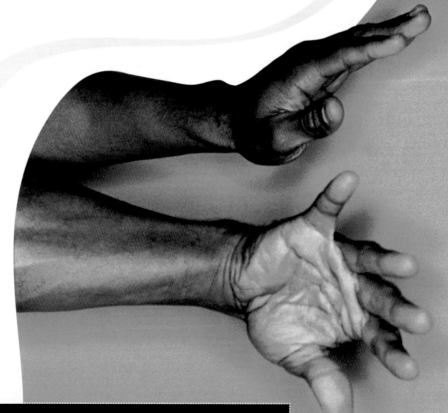

brain part of the body that controls thoughts and movement

▼ *Get ready to catch!*
Your brain tells you
how to do it.

Body messengers

You and your basketball teammates work together. You signal to one another. Signals tell each player what to do.

▼ *The player waits for a signal to pass the ball.*

Your body works like a team. Your body sends electrical signals (messages). These signals help your body parts work together. They move from one part of your body to another. They move through the **nervous system**. The nervous system is the part of your body that sends messages.

Special **cells** carry these messages. Cells are the building blocks from which living things are made. These special cells are **neurons**. Neurons carry messages. They tell different parts of your body how to work.

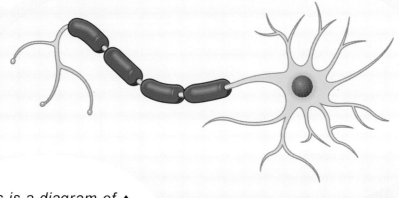

This is a diagram of ▲ a neuron. Neurons carry signals all around the body.

cells basic building blocks from which all living things are made
nervous system part of the body that sends messages

▼ A player passes the ball to his teammate.

Control box!

Most neurons are tiny. But some are very long. A giraffe has neurons that are 4.6 metres (15 feet) long. They stretch from its toe to its neck.

Message trail

You and your teammates try to move the ball. You pass the ball. You all work together.

To play basketball, your body must work like a team. You need your **nervous system**. It is your message system. It lets the parts of your body work together.

The nervous system is made up of **neurons**. Neurons carry messages all over the body. Thousands of tiny neurons join together to form **nerves**.

Nerves form pathways. The **brain** sends messages through these pathways. Some messages tell your muscles to work. Then, the muscles make your body move.

When neurons ▶ join together they form nerves.

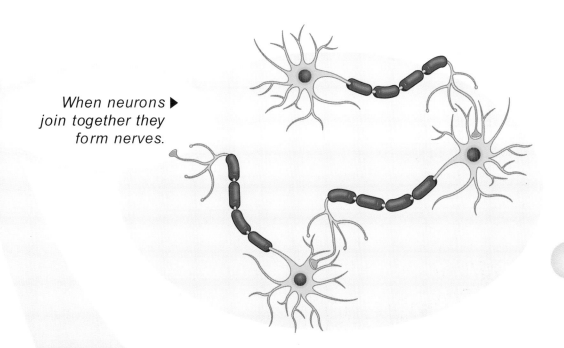

nerve bundle of neurons that connects the brain to different parts of the body

The coach

On a team the coach is in charge. The coach decides each player's job. Your body also has a coach. Your **brain** acts like a coach. It decides what your body does.

If a whistle blows during a game, you know to stop. Through practice, your brain has learned what a whistle means. It stores this information. When a whistle blows, your brain understands. It sends messages that tell your body to stop.

First the messages from your brain go down your **spinal cord**. The spinal cord runs down the middle of your back. It connects your brain to your body. Then, the messages travel to **nerves**. Nerves are made of tiny **neurons** (message carriers).

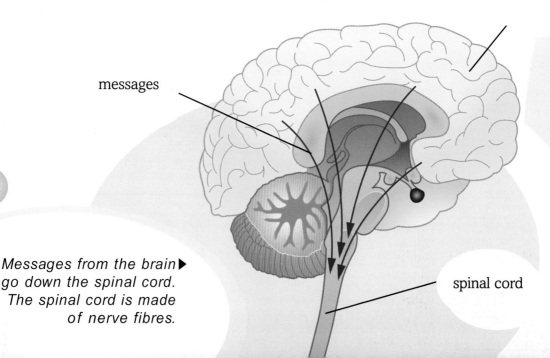

brain

messages

spinal cord

Messages from the brain ▶
go down the spinal cord.
The spinal cord is made
of nerve fibres.

▼ A coach often uses a whistle to send messages to players.

Finding out about the world

A coach tells each player what to do. In the same way, the **brain** instructs each part of your body.

First, your brain needs information. This information comes from **sense organs**. Your five senses are sight, hearing, smell, taste, and touch. Sense organs are the body parts that give you these senses.

The coach shouts out a game plan. Your ears hear the sound. A message is sent from your ears. It travels along a hearing **nerve**. The message is passed to your brain.

You see the coach waving his or her arms. Your eyes are sense organs. They send a message. The message travels along a seeing nerve. It goes to your **spinal cord**. Then, the message goes to your brain.

sense organ   part of the body that gets outside information

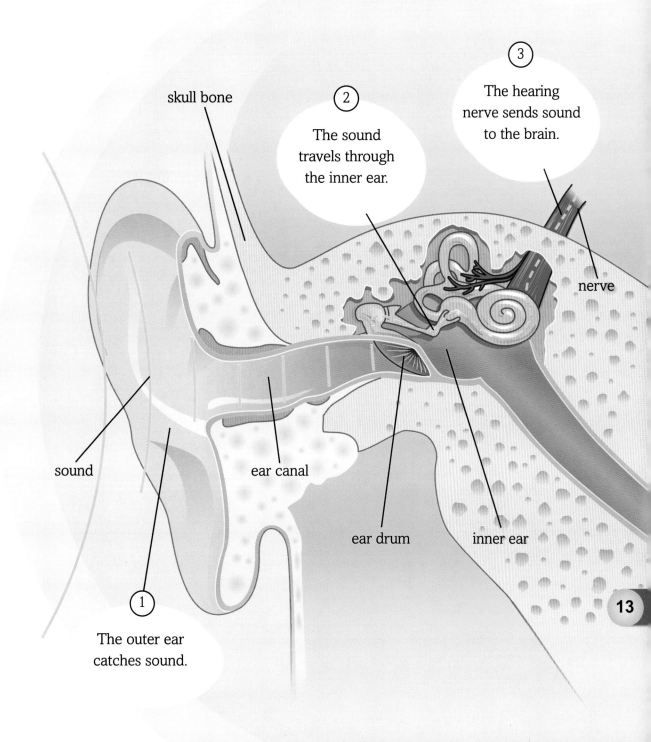

▼ *Ears send sound messages to the brain.*

skull bone

③ The hearing nerve sends sound to the brain.

② The sound travels through the inner ear.

nerve

sound

ear canal

ear drum

inner ear

① The outer ear catches sound.

13

Control centre

Different parts of the **brain** control different activities. The **cerebrum** is the largest part of the brain. It controls memory and movement. It controls thoughts and feelings. It is the part of the brain that solves problems.

You see a teammate signal to you. Your cerebrum reacts. It decides you should throw the ball. It sends messages to your muscles. Then, your muscles move.

The cerebrum has two halves. Each half controls different kinds of thoughts. The left half controls your speech. You use it to solve problems. It helps you remember things.

cerebrum

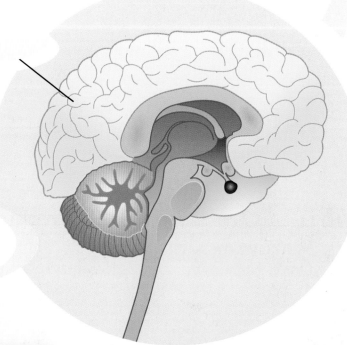

The cerebrum is ▶ the largest part of the brain.

cerebrum   largest part of the brain

The right half understands feelings. You use it when you draw pictures. You use it when you make up stories. You use it when you are feeling happy about the game.

A player aims for ▶ the basket. His brain decides when it is time to shoot.

A player shoots the ball. Muscles work together to shoot the ball through the hoop.

16

Working together

You catch a ball. You look up at the hoop. You bend your legs and arms. You jump. You shoot the ball.

Many muscles work together when you shoot the ball. Your **cerebrum** sends messages to your muscles. The messages tell your muscles to move.

But a different part of your **brain** also sends messages. It is the **cerebellum**. The cerebellum is under the cerebrum. It tells your muscles how to work together.

Without the cerebellum, you could not walk or run. Your muscles would not move in the right order. They would move too much or too little.

Cerebellum *means* ▶
"little brain".
The cerebellum is
much smaller than
the cerebrum.

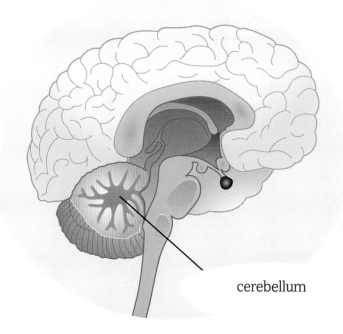

cerebellum

cerebellum   part of the brain under the cerebrum

Behind the scenes

You run, jump, and pass the ball. Your arm and leg muscles work hard. But you need more than fast legs and arms to play basketball.

Other parts of your body help. Muscles need **oxygen** to work. Oxygen is a gas in the air. Your lungs breathe in oxygen. Your heart moves oxygen around your body.

Your muscles also need **energy**. You need energy to make your body work. Your body gets energy from food. Your stomach breaks down food to get energy.

The **brain stem** controls all of this work. The brain stem is the lowest part of your **brain**. It sends signals to your lungs. It tells them to breathe deeply. It sends signals to your heart. It tells your heart to speed up or slow down. It also sends signals to your stomach. It tells it to break down food.

brain stem	lower part of the brain that connects with the spinal cord
energy	something you need to make your body work
oxygen	gas in the air

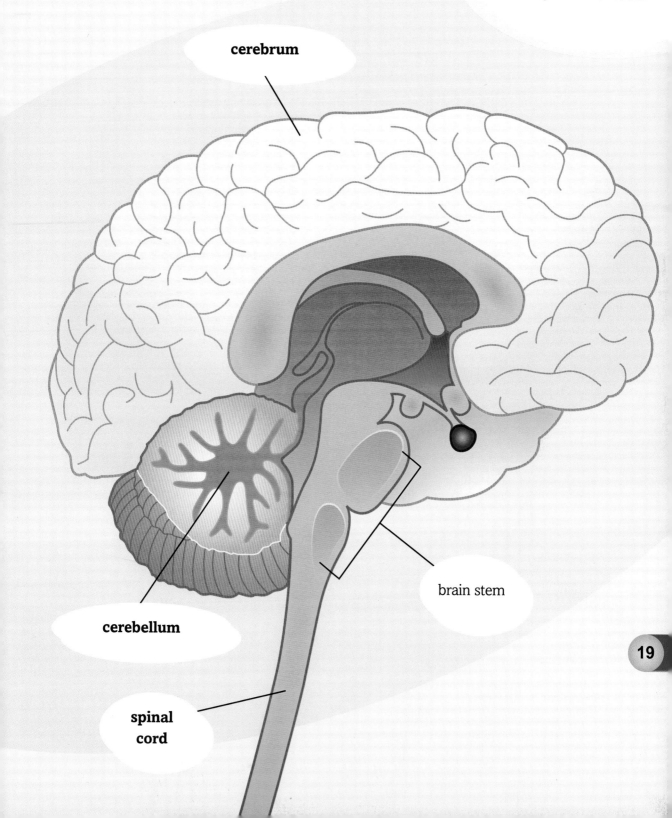

cerebrum

cerebellum

brain stem

spinal cord

The team

You catch the ball. You run down the court. Someone blocks your path. You pass the ball to a teammate. Your team works together to move the ball down the court.

All the parts of your **nervous system** are also working together. The first job is to get information. You get information from your **sense organs**.

▼ The ball touches your hand. Messages travel from your hand to your brain.

For example, you catch the ball with your hands. The pressure of the ball triggers your sense of touch. Your skin is a sense organ. Messages travel from **neurons** in your skin through **nerves**.

The nerves lead to the **spinal cord**. The messages travel up your spinal cord. They go to your **brain**. Now your brain knows you have caught the ball!

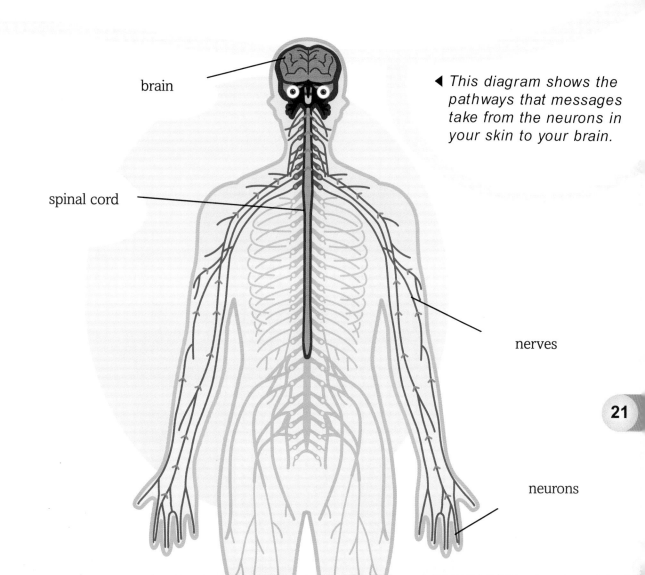

brain

spinal cord

nerves

neurons

◀ This diagram shows the pathways that messages take from the neurons in your skin to your brain.

Making a shot

You catch a ball and then look up. Your **brain** must decide what to do next.

Your eyes send signals to the brain. Your eyes see that you are near enough to score. Your brain decides you should try to shoot.

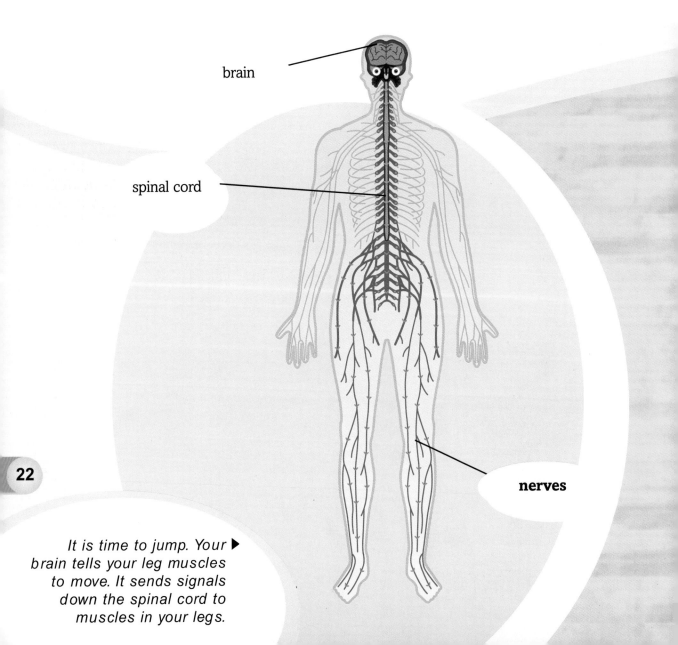

brain

spinal cord

nerves

It is time to jump. Your ▶ brain tells your leg muscles to move. It sends signals down the spinal cord to muscles in your legs.

How does your brain tell your body what to do?
Your brain sends messages. They travel down your
spinal cord. The messages tell your leg and arm
muscles to move. You bend your knees. You shoot
the ball. You score!

▲ *The crowd cheers when
the team works together
to score.*

Move fast!

You touch something sharp. Your hand jerks back. Oh no! There is broken glass on the basketball court.

Sometimes the body needs to react very quickly. There is no time for a message to go to the **brain** and back. Some actions happen without the brain's control. These actions are called **reflexes**. Reflexes keep you from getting hurt. They make you move quickly when there is danger.

If you touch something ▶ sharp, such as broken glass, you move fast! You pull your hand away.

Control box!

If a ball is thrown at you, you blink. You cannot stop your eyes from shutting. Blinking is a reflex that you cannot control.

reflex   action done without thought

Reflex messages do not have time to travel to your brain. The signals start with **nerves** in your skin. They speed directly to your **spinal cord**. Then messages race back to the muscles in your hand and arm. You jerk your hand back.

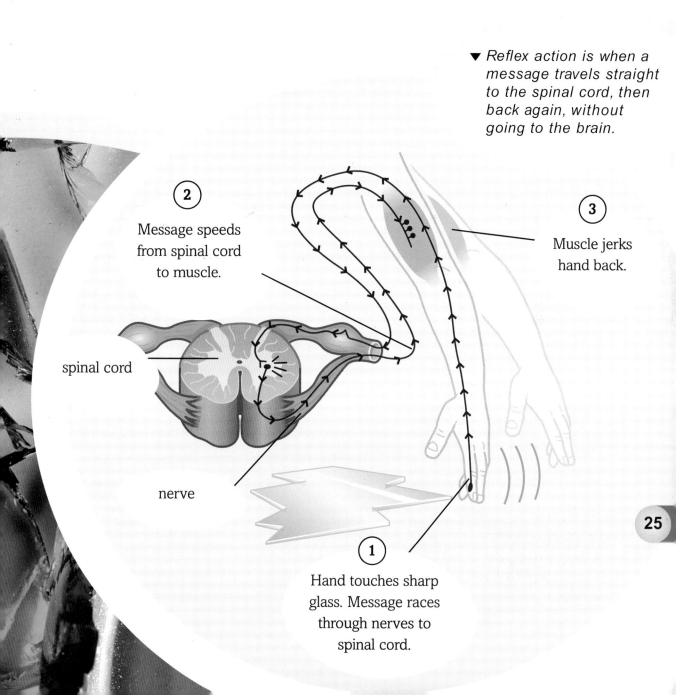

▼ Reflex action is when a message travels straight to the spinal cord, then back again, without going to the brain.

2
Message speeds from spinal cord to muscle.

3
Muscle jerks hand back.

spinal cord

nerve

1
Hand touches sharp glass. Message races through nerves to spinal cord.

Learning to be your best

As a baby you could not run or catch a ball. First, you learned to crawl. Then, you learned to walk and talk. Now, you can play sport. How do you learn new things?

Your **nervous system** is in charge of learning. When you learn something, this system stores new information. It makes new paths for sending messages. The paths link one **neuron** to the next. As you practise a new skill, the message goes over and over the new path.

With practice, the neurons stay linked. When neurons stay linked together, you have learned a new skill.

Control box!

It is easier to learn new skills when you are a child. After the age of 25, neurons start to die. It takes longer to learn something new. It is harder for neurons to form new links. So, you should learn as much as possible while you are young!

One neuron can be ▶ linked to thousands of others.

▼ *Practising teaches your neurons to make a new path.*

Brain bits

Remember . . .

The **brain** is the control centre of the body. The brain controls thinking, speaking, learning, moving, balancing, breathing, and more.

Neurons carry messages all around the body. They link together to form **nerves**. Nerves connect the brain to other parts of the body.

Sense organs get information about the world. They send messages to the brain. Ears and eyes are sense organs.

Neurons carry messages to and from the brain. Babies have a lot of neurons. They grow 250,000 neurons each minute before they are born.

Humans have big brains. A baby's brain weighs more than a lion's brain. A human adult's brain weighs about 1.4 kilograms (3 pounds). But an elephant's brain is even bigger. It weighs about 6 kilograms (13 pounds).

The nose is a sense organ. Dogs find out about the world through their noses. Most dogs have one billion neurons for smelling. That is 80 times more smelling neurons than humans have! Bloodhounds have about four billion smelling neurons. They can smell scent trails that are up to four days old!

Glossary

brain part of the body that controls thoughts and movement. The brain is the control centre of the body.

brain stem lower part of the brain that connects with the spinal cord. It controls heart rate, breathing, food processing, and swallowing.

cells basic building blocks from which all living things are made. Nerves and muscles are made from cells.

cerebellum part of the brain under the cerebrum. It makes muscles work together and controls balance.

cerebrum largest part of the brain. It controls movement, thoughts, memories, and feelings.

energy something you need to make your body work. You get your energy from food.

nerve bundle of neurons that connects the brain to different parts of the body. Nerves carry messages to all parts of the body.

nervous system part of the body that sends messages. The brain, spinal cord, and nerves make up the nervous system.

neuron cell that carries messages. Neurons link together to make nerves.

oxygen gas in the air. When you breathe, you take in oxygen.

reflex action done without thought. The brain does not control reflex actions.

sense organ part of the body that gets outside information. The eyes, ears, nose, tongue, and skin are sense organs.

spinal cord thick cord that connects the brain to other nerves. The spinal cord carries messages to and from the brain.

Want to know more?

Books to read

- *Body Focus: Brain*, Steve Parker (Heinemann Library, 2004)

- *How My Body Works: Brain*, Anita Ganeri (Evans Brothers, 2006)

- *Why Should I Go To Bed Now? And other questions about a healthy mind*, Louise Spilsbury (Heinemann Library, 2004)

Websites

- http://www.cartage.org.lb/en/kids/science/Biology%20Cells/Nervous%20System/introb.html
  Learn more about how the nervous system and the brain work together.

- http://yucky.kids.discovery.com/noflash/body/pg000136.html
  More interesting facts about the nervous system and how it works.

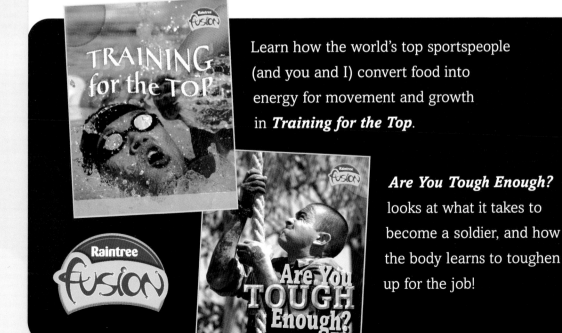

Learn how the world's top sportspeople (and you and I) convert food into energy for movement and growth in *Training for the Top*.

Are You Tough Enough? looks at what it takes to become a soldier, and how the body learns to toughen up for the job!

Index

babies 26, 28, 29

basketball 4, 6, 9, 15, 16, 17, 18, 23

blinking 24

brain 4, 5, 7, 9, 10, 12, 13, 14, 18, 21, 22, 23, 24, 25, 28, 29

brain stem 18, 19

cells 7

cerebellum 17, 19

cerebrum 14–15, 17, 19

coaches 10, 11, 12

dogs 29

ears 12, 13

elephants 29

emotions 14, 15

energy 18

eyes 4, 12, 22

giraffes 8

learning 26, 28

muscles 4, 9, 14, 16, 17, 18, 22, 23, 25

nerve fibres 10

nerves 9, 10, 12, 21, 25, 28

nervous system 7, 9, 10, 20, 26

neurons 7, 8, 9, 10, 21, 23, 26, 27, 28, 29

noses 29

oxygen 18

problem solving 14

reflexes 24, 25

sense organs 12, 20, 21, 28, 29

signals (messages) 7, 9, 10, 12, 14, 18, 21, 22, 23, 24, 25, 26, 28

speech 14

spinal cord 10, 11, 19, 21, 23, 25

teammates 4, 6, 9, 14, 20, 23

thoughts 14